MW01181236

Delaware
Facts and Symbols

by Elaine A. Kule

Consultant:
Tom Summers
Coordinator of Public Programming
Delaware Public Archives

Hilltop Books

an imprint of Capstone Press
Mankato, Minnesota

Hilltop Books are published by Capstone Press
151 Good Counsel Drive, P.O. Box 669, Mankato, Minnesota 56002
http://www.capstone-press.com

Library of Congress Cataloging-in-Publication Data
Kule, Elaine A.
   Delaware facts and symbols/by Elaine A. Kule.
   p. cm.—(The states and their symbols)
   Includes bibliographical references and index.
   Summary: Presents information about the state of Delaware, its nickname, motto,
and emblems.
   ISBN 0-7368-0635-0
   1. Emblems, State—Delaware—Juvenile literature. 2. Delaware—Miscellanea—
Juvenile literature. [1. Emblems, State—Delaware. 2. Delaware.] I. Title. II. Series
CR203.D45 K85 2001
975.1—dc21   00-020878

Editorial Credits
Erika Mikkelson, editor; Linda Clavel, production designer and illustrator;
   Heidi Schoof and Kimberly Danger, photo researchers

Photo Credits
Bruce D. Flaig, cover
Delaware Office of Tourism, 12
Dr. Charles Steinmetz, Jr., 18
Frederick D. Atwood, 6, 14
One Mile Up, Inc., 8, 10 (inset)
Richard Demler, 22 (top, middle)
Unicorn Stock Photos/Martha McBride, 16; Jeff Greenberg, 22 (bottom)
Visuals Unlimited/Dick Keen, 10; Kevin and Betty Collins, 20

State seal on page 8 used by permission of the Delaware Public Archives.

1 2 3 4 5 6 06 05 04 03 02 01

Table of Contents

Map 4
Fast Facts 5
State Name and Nickname 7
State Seal and Motto 9
State Capitol and Flag 11
State Bird 13
State Tree 15
State Flower 17
State Fish 19
More State Symbols 21

Places to Visit 22
Words to Know 23
Read More 23
Useful Addresses 24
Internet Sites 24
Index 24

Fast Facts

Capital: Dover is the capital of Delaware.

Largest City: Wilmington is the largest city in Delaware. More than 72,000 people live in this city.

Size: Delaware covers 1,955 square miles (5,063 square kilometers). It is the 49th largest state.

Location: Delaware lies midway along the east coast of the United States.

Population: 753,538 people live in Delaware (U.S. Census Bureau, 1999 estimate).

Statehood: On December 7, 1787, Delaware became the first state to join the United States.

Natural Resources: Soil, fish, and minerals are important natural resources in Delaware.

Manufactured Goods: Workers in Delaware make chemicals, food products, and paper products.

Crops: Delaware farmers grow soybeans and corn. They also raise chickens and dairy cattle.

In 1610, Samuel Argall sailed into what is now Delaware Bay. Argall named the area after Lord de la Warr. Lord de la Warr was the first governor of the Virginia colony. Delaware gets it name from the Delaware Bay.

Delaware has many nicknames. One name is The First State. Delaware was the first state to ratify the U.S. Constitution in 1787. Another nickname is The Diamond State. President Thomas Jefferson once said Delaware was a jewel among states.

People also call Delaware the Blue Hen State. Delaware earned this nickname during the Revolutionary War (1775-1783). Soldiers staged fights between chickens. Delaware soldiers used blue hen chickens in these fights. These birds and Delaware's soldiers were strong fighters.

Delaware's newest nickname is Small Wonder. Delaware's size and beauty give it this nickname.

President Thomas Jefferson saw that Delaware's location on the east coast was ideal for shipping. He called Delaware a jewel among states.

State Seal and Motto

Delaware officials adopted the state seal on January 17, 1777. The words "Great Seal of the State of Delaware" surround the seal. The years 1793, 1847, and 1907 appear at the bottom of the seal. State officials made changes to the seal during these years.

Delaware's seal shows pictures of farming and businesses important to the state. A shield is in the center of the seal. The shield shows pictures of an ox, a bundle of wheat, and corn. These symbols represent farming. A militiaman and a farmer stand on opposite sides of the shield. The militiaman represents the need for citizens to help protect their country. The farmer shows the importance of farming. A sailing ship sits above the shield. It represents Delaware's shipping and transportation businesses.

Delaware's state motto, "Liberty and Independence," lies below the shield. Delaware officials adopted the motto and added it to the state seal in 1847.

The water above the ox on Delaware's state seal stands for the Delaware River.

DECEMBER 7, 1787

State Capitol and Flag

Dover is the capital of Delaware. Delaware's capitol building is in Dover. Government officials meet there to make the state's laws.

Delaware has had two state capitol buildings. The State House in Dover was the capitol from 1792 to 1933. Some government offices are still located in the State House. Workers completed the current capitol building in 1933. The building is called Legislative Hall.

Delaware's government adopted the state flag on July 24, 1913. The flag's colors are colonial blue and buff, a light tan color. These colors were on George Washington's military uniform.

A diamond with pictures from the state seal is in the center of the flag. The date December 7, 1787 appears below the diamond. On that day, Delaware became the first state in the United States to approve the U.S. Constitution.

Legislative Hall in Dover is Delaware's capitol building.

State Bird

Delaware officials named the blue hen chicken the state bird on April 14, 1939. During the Revolutionary War, Delaware's soldiers enjoyed watching certain chickens fight. The birds slashed each other with their claws. The strongest birds were blue hen chickens.

The Delaware soldiers fought the British as hard as the chickens fought. The soldiers' bravery earned them the nickname, "the blue hen's chickens."

Blue hen chickens are similar to other chickens. They do not have teeth. They use their sharp bills to cut food. Blue hen chickens are different from other chickens because they have blue feathers.

This chicken may be descended from blue hen chickens.

State Tree

The American holly became Delaware's state tree on May 1, 1939. Olive Wilkins suggested the tree. She worked for State Forester William S. Taber. Wilkins spoke to him about the tree's beauty. The legislature soon declared the American holly Delaware's state tree.

The American holly grows throughout Delaware. The tree has dark green, thorny leaves and red berries. The tree can grow up to 60 feet (18 meters) tall. Its trunk can reach 20 inches (51 centimeters) in diameter. The tree's bark is light gray, thin, and smooth.

The American holly is important to Delaware. Some people create wreaths from the branches and berries during the holiday season. The American holly sometimes is called Christmas holly or evergreen holly.

Red berries grow on the branches of American holly trees.

State Flower

Delaware officials named the peach blossom the state flower in 1895. Farmers and schoolchildren suggested the peach blossom. Officials chose the flower because people sometimes called Delaware the Peach State. Delaware's orchards once grew more than 800,000 peach trees.

Peach blossoms bloom in early spring. They appear before the tree's dark green leaves bud. Peach blossoms can be white, pink, or red. The blossoms usually have five petals. Peach blossoms grow to be 1 to 2 inches (2.5 to 5 centimeters) wide.

Peaches grow on the trees after the flowers bloom and drop off the tree. This fruit is white, yellow, or red. The outside of the peach is fuzzy. A pit, or seed, is inside the fruit. People often eat peaches with cream or bake them in pies.

Peach blossoms can be white, pink, or red.

State Fish

State officials named the weakfish the state fish in 1981. Weakfish have dark yellow-green or blue bodies and dark spots. The fish grow to be 1 to 3 feet (30 to 90 centimeters) long.

People fish for weakfish off Delaware's coast. The best time to catch weakfish is between May and November. Weakfish live in shallow ocean water and travel in large groups.

The weakfish gets its name because its mouth tears when it is hooked. People must then lift the weakfish onto the boat using a net.

People call the weakfish by many other names. Sea trout, gray trout, yellow mouth, and yellow fin trout are all names for the weakfish. Some people also call the weakfish squeteague (skwi-TEEG) or tiderunner.

Weakfish live in the Atlantic Ocean near Delaware's coast.

State Beverage: Milk is Delaware's state beverage. State officials adopted this drink in 1983. Officials chose milk because it is a healthy drink. Farmers in Delaware raise dairy cows.

State Bug: In 1974, a class of second-graders wrote letters to Delaware lawmakers. They wanted the ladybug to be the state bug. The lawmakers followed the students' advice and adopted the symbol on April 25, 1974.

State Colors: Delaware's state colors are colonial blue and buff. General George Washington's military uniform was made of these colors. Delaware's state flag also is colonial blue and buff.

State Mineral: In March 1977, officials named sillimanite the state mineral. The Delaware Mineralogical Society suggested the mineral. Sillimanite is white, brown, and green. The mineral is found in aluminum-rich rock in Delaware.

Like all beetles, ladybugs have six legs and two wings.

Places to Visit

Bombay Hook National Wildlife Refuge

The Bombay Hook National Wildlife Refuge is in Kent County. The refuge has walking trails, observation towers, and an auto tour. Visitors to the refuge watch ducks, geese, and a variety of other wildlife.

Constitution Corner Park

Constitution Corner Park is in Dover near State Street. A monument stands in the park to honor Delaware's signing of the U.S. Constitution. The entire document is engraved on a big metal cube. A large bronze feather pen rests on the cube.

Delaware Seashore State Park

Delaware Seashore State Park is one of Delaware's four beach parks. This site is located south of Rehoboth Beach. Six miles (10 kilometers) of beaches are available for swimming, surfing, camping, and fishing.

Words to Know

buff (BUFF)—a light tan color
Constitution (kon-stuh-TOO-shun)—the written document containing the laws by which the United States is governed
militiaman (mi-LISH-a-MAN)—a citizen soldier
monument (MON-u-ment)—a statue or building made to honor a person or an event
orchard (ORCH-erd)—a large area of fruit trees
pit (PIT)—a large, hard seed in the middle of some fruits
ratify (RA-ti-fy)—to agree to something

Read More

Blashfield, Jean F. *Delaware.* America the Beautiful. New York: Children's Press, 2000.

Kummer, Patricia K. *Delaware.* One Nation. Mankato, Minn.: Capstone Books, 1999.

Schuman, Michael. *Delaware.* Celebrate the States. New York: Benchmark Books, 2000.

Usel, T. M. *George Washington.* Photo-Illustrated Biographies. Mankato, Minn.: Bridgestone Books, 1996.

Useful Addresses

Delaware Tourism Office
99 Kings Highway
Dover, DE 19901

**Historical Society of
  Delaware**
505 Market Street
Wilmington, DE 19801

Internet Sites

Delaware Facts and History
http://www.state.de.us/facts/history/delfact.htm
Delaware State Parks Online
http://www.destateparks.com
Stately Knowledge: Delaware: Just the Facts
http://www.ipl.org/youth/stateknow/de1.html

Index

American holly, 15
Argall, Samuel, 7
blue hen chicken, 7, 13
de la Warr, Lord, 7
Jefferson, Thomas, 7
ladybug, 21
Legislative Hall, 11

militiaman, 9
milk, 21
peach blossom, 17
sillimanite, 21
Washington, George, 11, 21
weakfish, 19
Wilkins, Olive, 15